CAREER EXPLORATION

Fashion Designer

by Rosemary Wallner

Consultant:
Lisa Smilor
Executive Assistant and
Manager, Scholarship Programs
Council of Fashion Designers of America

CAPSTONE BOOKS

an imprint of Capstone Press
Mankato, Minnesota

Capstone Books are published by Capstone Press
151 Good Counsel Drive, P.O. Box 669, Mankato, Minnesota 56002
http://www.capstone-press.com

Library of Congress Cataloging-in-Publication Data
Wallner, Rosemary, 1964–
    Fashion designer/by Rosemary Wallner.
    p. cm.—(Career exploration)
    Includes bibliographical references and index.
    Summary: Introduces the career of fashion designer, providing information
about personal and educational requirements, daily activities, salary, employment
outlook, and possible future positions.
    ISBN 0-7368-0595-8
    1. Costume design—Vocational guidance—Juvenile literature. [1. Fashion
designer. 2. Vocational guidance.] I. Title. II. Series.
TT507 .W21735 2001
746.9'2'023—dc21   00-021582

Editorial Credits
Leah K. Pockrandt, editor; Steve Christensen, cover designer; Kia Bielke, production
    designer and illustrator; Heidi Schoof and Kimberly Danger, photo researchers

Photo Credits
David F. Clobes, cover, 6, 9 10, 13, 14, 16, 18, 22, 31, 32, 34, 43, 46
FPG International LLC, 28
International Stock/Patrick Ramsey, 25
Unicorn Stock Photos/Florent Flipper, 21, 37, 40; Larry Stanley, 39

**Special thanks to staff and students of the Clothing Design Program,
Department of Design, Housing and Apparel, College of Human Ecology,
University of Minnesota, for their assistance with this book.**

1 2 3 4 5 6 06 05 04 03 02 01

Table of Contents

Fast Facts

Career Title	Fashion Designer
O*NET Number	34038A
DOT Cluster (Dictionary of Occupational Titles)	Professional, technical, and managerial occupations
DOT Number	142.061-018
GOE Number (Guide for Occupational Exploration)	01.02.03
NOC Number (National Occupational Classification-Canada)	524
Salary Range (U.S. Bureau of Labor Statistics and Human Resources Development Canada, late 1990s figures)	U.S.: $13,780 to more than $1 million Canada: $10,000 to more than $1 million (Canadian dollars)
Minimum Educational Requirements	U.S.: associate's or bachelor's degree Canada: associate's or bachelor's degree
Certification/Licensing Requirements	U.S.: none Canada: none

Subject Knowledge	Figure drawing and flat sketching; design concepts; garment construction; fabric; fine arts; art history; sales and marketing
Personal Abilities/Skills	Understand and apply artistic principles and techniques; visualize the final product from rough sketches or work drawings; use pens or charcoal skillfully to produce accurate designs; choose the most appropriate fabric to express an idea or create a particular effect
Job Outlook	U.S.: faster than average growth Canada: poor
Personal Interests	Artistic: interest in creative expression of feelings or ideas
Similar Types of Jobs	Visual artist; textiles designer; home furnishings designer; architect; landscape architect; photographer; merchandise displayer; interior designer

Chapter 1

Fashion Designer

Fashion designers create clothing designs. They use different fabrics and other materials to create new styles of clothing for people to buy.

The Seventh Avenue garment district is the center of the North American fashion industry. Seventh Avenue is located in New York City's Manhattan area. Many clothing manufacturers, designers, showrooms, and design schools are located in this area.

What Fashion Designers Do

Most fashion designers create clothes that follow fashion trends. Designers must know these current fashion styles. A fashion designer's reputation is important. Designers who do not follow current fashion trends may have low sales. This will hurt their reputations.

Fashion designers create a variety of designs.

Many fashion designers specialize in certain types of clothing design. For example, some fashion designers create sportswear designs. They design casual clothes such as shorts, pants, and sweaters. Some designers create bridal gowns and other wedding clothes.

Other designers create accessories. They design belts, jewelry, and scarves. Some accessory designers specialize in shoes, socks, or handbags.

Still other designers are costume designers. They create designs for theater, TV, or movie productions.

Fashion designers often work in noisy, cluttered workrooms. They may work at design tables or at long cutting tables. Designers and other staff members cut out clothing pieces using patterns on cutting tables. Fashion designers stand much of the day.

Fashion designers often work with other workroom staff members. The workroom staff may include a head designer, assistant designer, and one or two sample makers. In large firms, head designers may have one or more assistant

Fashion designers may work at design or cutting tables.

designers. Assistant designers help head designers during each step of the design process. Sample makers sew samples of a designer's work.

Types of Fashion Designers

Some fashion designers create clothes for celebrities or other wealthy people. These designers display their work at fashion shows. These shows often take place in large cities such

Fashion designers often work with other designers, pattern cutters, or sewers.

as Paris and New York. But only a small number of fashion designers show their designs this way. Most fashion designers create and adapt fashions for sale to the general public.

Most fashion designers work for apparel manufacturers. These companies make and sell clothes and accessories to stores. They also sell directly to customers through catalogs. Fashion designers at such companies create a variety of designs. They sometimes base their work on the designs of well-known designers.

Apparel manufacturer designers often create clothes in several sizes. They also may design 25 to 100 or more styles for each collection. A collection also is called a clothing line. A line of clothing is specific to a fashion season.

Most companies or designers present four apparel collections each year. They show one collection each season. But some designers show only two collections each year.

Working in Other Areas

Some fashion designers are self-employed. These designers create custom-made clothes for different clients. The clothes may be original creations for clients or part of the designers' lines or collections.

Some fashion designers work for specialty stores or high-fashion department stores. They design original garments for sale in the store.

A Career as a Fashion Designer

Fashion designers usually begin their careers as assistant designers. These designers perform a variety of tasks. They may fit designs on models or cut out and sew samples. They may make sure fabrics are the right colors and patterns. Assistant designers also sketch design ideas. They learn a great deal about the fashion business as they work.

Fashion designers may earn more responsibilities after working in the business for several years. In many companies, these designers can create part of a line or simple clothing pieces. They also may work with workroom staff and advertising employees.

Fashion designers with 10 years of experience usually work in one design area. These designers may schedule lines. They may search for new, talented designers to hire. They may oversee and teach these designers.

Many designers create original garments for sale.

Current Trends

Fashion designers want to create new designs or
trends. Designers who create new trends often
become well known. But most designers watch
the work of other designers to keep up with
trends. Designers also watch people to see the
clothes and accessories they like to wear.

Fashion designers read fashion magazines and other publications to keep up with design trends.

Fashion designers find a variety of ways to keep up with design trends. They read fashion magazines. They read newspapers and other publications that show current trends. Fashion designers attend fashion shows to see what other designers are creating. Designers also attend fabric shows twice a year to see the different fabrics that are available.

Fashion Designers' Schedules

Fashion designers who work for manufacturing companies or design firms generally work regular daytime hours. They may need to adjust their workdays to suit their clients. They may meet with their clients during the evenings or weekends. They may have meetings in their own offices or at clients' homes or offices. Fashion designers may travel to other cities to check on showrooms or factories.

Self-employed fashion designers also must adjust their hours to meet their clients' needs. These fashion designers work hard to find and keep clients. They usually cannot afford to hire assistants or other help.

Fashion designers work the hardest right before production deadlines or fashion shows. They must complete their designs. They then must make sure sewers can complete the garments in time for the deadlines or shows.

Chapter 2

Day-to-Day Activities

Fashion designers' daily activities vary. But most designers complete their projects in similar ways.

Research and Sketches

Fashion designers start with ideas for garments or accessories. They perform research to see if these ideas will appeal to the public. Fashion designers visit stores to see the styles of clothes people buy. They visit nightclubs to see what people wear. They study the clothes people wear to relax or to business, sports, and other special events.

Fashion designers select fabrics for their garments. Different fabrics give clothes the fit or texture designers want. Designers use one type of

Fashion designers have a variety of daily duties such as selecting fabric for garments.

Some fashion designers use computers to create their designs.

fabric for swimwear. They use another type for bridal gowns and other formal wear.

Fashion designers research the best fabric to use for their designs. They visit art museums and fashion shows. They visit textile companies where fabrics are made.

Specialty fashion designers must determine the needs of the people who buy their clothes. They must design clothes in the styles and colors that people want. For example, people who buy sportswear may want a jacket to wear on cold days. Young adults may want colorful shirts or pants. Designers perform research to find new ideas for their designs.

Fashion designers make hundreds of sketches to record and develop their ideas. They first draw rough sketches. These drawings show only the garments' basic shapes. Designers often draw croquis. These small sketches help designers work through different thoughts during the design process.

Designers then draw more detailed flat sketches. These sketches show the specifications of the designs. Specifications include the fabric colors and patterns. They also include buttons, zippers, and other items.

Some fashion designers use computers to create their designs. They use a system called computer-aided design (CAD). Fashion designers use CAD to show different clothing styles, colors, and fabrics on computer monitors. They can make changes to the designs on screen. They then can print out their final designs.

Patterns, Mockups, and Samples

Fashion designers create pattern pieces after the designs are finished. They draw the proper sizes of the patterns on paper. Some designers use CAD to help them size and print patterns. Other designers use rulers, pencils, and long sheets of paper to make patterns.

Fashion designers follow patterns when cutting out the garment pieces. Designers lay the pattern pieces on lengths of muslin. This lightweight cotton fabric is inexpensive. Fashion designers use muslin to sew mockups. Designers use the mockups to work out the fit and finishing touches on the garments. Using mockups allows designers to save their more expensive fabrics for the samples.

Fashion designers then use the selected fabrics to make the final sample garments based on their designs. Designers check samples carefully. They make sure people will be able to get the garments on and off easily. They make sure the fabrics fit the designs.

Showing Garments

Fashion designers show their garments to people at manufacturing companies. Manufacturers

Fashion designers display their designs at shows.

mass-produce clothes. They make thousands of copies of different garments.

Many fashion designers host runway shows. They use these shows to display their ideas. Models wear the garments and walk down a long stage called a runway. Fashion designers usually host two shows a year. TV reporters and newspaper and magazine writers attend the shows. Representatives from department stores and apparel or accessory manufacturing companies also attend the shows.

Chapter 3

The Right Candidate

Fashion designers need a variety of artistic and technical skills. Designers must be creative and imaginative. They must communicate their ideas both visually and verbally.

Interests

Fashion designers must be interested in clothing and accessories. They should know a great deal about fashion and style. They must understand colors and shapes and how they work together. Fashion designers should be able to put clothes and accessories together in imaginative ways.

Fashion designers must be observant. They should be quick to recognize fashion trends. They should pay attention to the fashions displayed in stores. They should observe what people wear.

Fashion designers need to know how colors and shapes work together.

Fashion designers try to be original. They want to be the first to create a new design or solve a fashion problem. Their ideas must be new, unusual, and pleasing.

Work Styles

Fashion designers must use both verbal and visual communication skills. They must be able to talk with others and describe their designs. They must be able to show their designs through sketches and samples.

Fashion designers need self-discipline. They must start projects on their own and manage their time. They must meet deadlines and production schedules. Companies want designers who can work on many tasks with little supervision.

Fashion designers must be able to work with others. They usually work as part of design teams. They work with assistant designers, pattern cutters, sewers, and advertising representatives. Fashion designers also discuss their ideas and designs with sales representatives and clients.

Fashion designers often work as part of design teams.

Basic Skills

Fashion designers must have good problem-solving abilities. They need to visualize how final products will look. They must be able to picture how the clothes they design will look on people.

Fashion designers must be artistic. They use paintbrushes, pens, and charcoal to create design sketches. They learn different artistic techniques such as painting with gouache. Designers use this

Workplace Skills   Yes / No

Resources:
Assign use of time .... ☑ ☐
Assign use of money .... ☑ ☐
Assign use of material and facility resources .... ☑ ☐
Assign use of human resources .... ☑ ☐

Interpersonal Skills:
Take part as a member of a team .... ☑ ☐
Teach others .... ☑ ☐
Serve clients/customers .... ☑ ☐
Show leadership .... ☑ ☐
Work with others to arrive at a decision .... ☑ ☐
Work with a variety of people .... ☑ ☐

Information:
Acquire and judge information .... ☑ ☐
Understand and follow legal requirements .... ☑ ☐
Organize and maintain information .... ☑ ☐
Understand and communicate information .... ☑ ☐
Use computers to process information .... ☑ ☐

Systems:
Identify, understand, and work with systems .... ☑ ☐
Understand environmental, social, political, economic,
        or business systems .... ☑ ☐
Oversee and correct system performance .... ☐ ☑
Improve and create systems .... ☐ ☑

Technology:
Select technology .... ☑ ☐
Apply technology to task .... ☑ ☐
Maintain and troubleshoot technology .... ☐ ☑

Foundation Skills

Basic Skills:
Read .... ☑ ☐
Write .... ☑ ☐
Do arithmetic and math .... ☑ ☐
Speak and listen .... ☑ ☐

Thinking Skills:
Learn .... ☑ ☐
Reason .... ☑ ☐
Think creatively .... ☑ ☐
Make decisions .... ☑ ☐
Solve problems .... ☑ ☐

Personal Qualities:
Take individual responsibility .... ☑ ☐
Have self-esteem and self-management .... ☑ ☐
Be sociable .... ☑ ☐
Be fair, honest, and sincere .... ☑ ☐

paint to color their sketches. Gouache allows designers to make the colors in the sketches as sheer or as dark as needed. Designers also use computers and special design software. They must have good arm and hand steadiness.

Fashion designers must know a great deal about color. They must be able to match different colors of fabrics together on garments. They must know the basic color wheel. The color wheel shows many different colors and how the colors relate to each other.

Fashion designers must be able to listen to other people's opinions. They know that tastes in style and fashion change quickly. Fashion designers also must be able to learn from criticism. Some people may not like the designs fashion designers create. Designers can use these suggestions to make the garments better.

Fashion designers who want to start their own businesses must have good business skills. They must know how to market clothes. They must know who to show their ideas to. Fashion designers also must know how to hire people and manage money.

Chapter 4

Preparing for the Career

Most fashion designers train to learn or improve the skills necessary for the career. Many companies prefer to hire fashion designers with some formal education and training.

High School Education

Students who want to become fashion designers should take a variety of classes. Art, model drawing, and business classes are helpful to designers. Students learn how to draw body shapes in model drawing classes. This skill will help fashion designers draw clothing designs.

Fashion designers must have a variety of art and design skills.

Students also should take communications and computer classes.

Students should find ways to use their design interest. They should look for opportunities to be creative. Students can help create costumes and sets for school performances. They can design posters for school clubs and programs.

Students should keep croquis books. They can use these sketchbooks to draw designs or sketch ideas. Students can keep samples of ribbons, fabrics, or photos in their sketchbooks.

Students also should start portfolios. People put copies of their designs and other art in these books or folders. A portfolio contains a person's best work. Students show their portfolios to get accepted into a design program at a college or university. School instructors study the work to see if the students have talent for fashion design.

Post-Secondary Education

Most designers earn a degree from a fashion design school. Some fashion design schools

Students can gain experience by creating costumes for school performances.

offer both an associate's degree and a bachelor's degree. Other fashion design schools offer either an associate's degree or a bachelor's degree. Most students earn an associate's degree in two years. It usually takes a student about four years to earn a bachelor's degree. Both degree programs offer a variety of courses in fashion design.

Fashion design students work with teachers to improve their skills.

In Canada, fashion design students can earn a design program diploma or a bachelor's degree. A program diploma is similar to an associate's degree.

Design students study a variety of fashion design subjects. Students take classes in sketching, patternmaking, and textiles. In textiles classes, students learn about the different types of fabrics used to make clothes. They learn about the materials used to make accessories. Fashion design students also study design marketing. They learn about art history and costume history. Most students also learn how to use CAD systems.

Some students choose a design specialty. These students focus their studies on one area of fashion design. Specialties include formalwear, accessories, swimwear, and children's wear.

Students also take business classes. These classes include manufacturing and merchandising. Manufacturing classes teach students about the process of turning designs into finished products. Merchandising classes teach students how to sell their designs through newspaper, magazine, and TV advertisements.

Some students show their designs in fashion shows. Schools may sponsor a student show at the end of each school year. Students create samples of their designs to display in the show. Professional fashion designers sometimes attend student shows. Designers look for new, talented designers to hire.

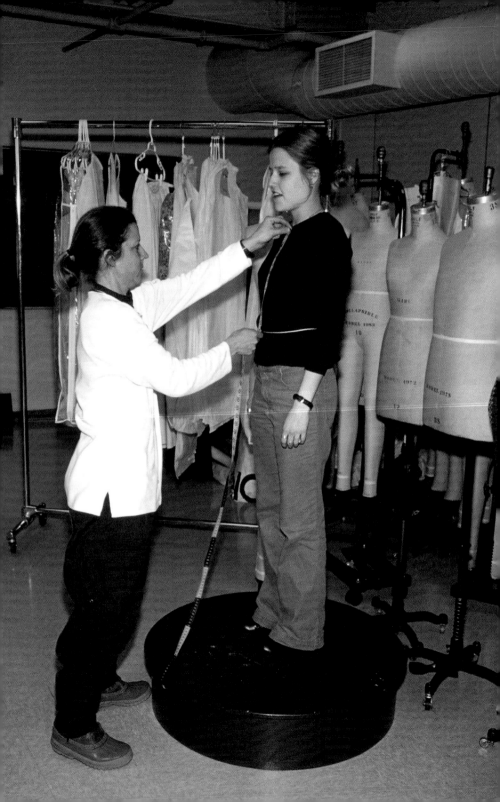

Chapter 5

The Market

The job outlook for fashion designers is good. Fashion and style continue to be popular around the world. Designers will be needed to create new designs for consumers.

Salary

In the United States, full-time fashion designers earn between $13,780 and $1 million or more per year. Well-known fashion designers usually earn the highest wages. Starting salaries for most fashion designers are between $21,000 and $30,000 per year. The low end of the salary range is based on a group average by the U.S. Bureau of Labor Statistics. This salary group also includes floral designers, interior designers, furniture designers, textile designers, and set designers. The high end

Fashion designers have many job opportunities.

of the salary range is from other sources in the fashion industry.

In Canada, full-time fashion designers earn from $10,000 to $1 million or more per year. Most fashion designers earn between $29,500 and $49,800 per year. The low end of the salary range is based on a group average determined by Human Resources Development Canada. This salary group also includes graphic designers, interior designers, theater designers, craftspersons, and pattern makers. The high end of the salary range is from other sources in the fashion industry.

Fashion designers' salaries vary depending on different factors. Designers with more skills, talent, and experience earn more money than new fashion designers. Salaries also vary depending on fashion designers' specialties.

Fashion designers' salaries also depend on where they work. Fashion designers in large cities such as New York, London, and Paris often earn higher salaries. Designers often have better job opportunities in these cities. Many fashion companies are located in these cities.

Creative designers have the best chance of succeeding.

Job Outlook

Fashion designers with talent and an education will have long careers in the design business. People who lack creativity will find it difficult to establish and maintain a career in fashion design.

In the United States, the fashion industry is expected to have faster than average growth. Fashion designers will be needed to replace those who leave the field. Some designers do not like how many hours they must work. But fashion designers will have competition for jobs. Many talented people will be competing for few job openings. In Canada, the employment outlook is poor.

The demand for fashion designers should rise in the United States. Fashion designers will be needed as consumers become more concerned with fashion and style. People often want to purchase better-quality clothes as they earn higher salaries. Many fashion designers will be needed to satisfy the needs of a variety of consumers.

Advancement Opportunities

Fashion designers may have many advancement opportunities throughout their careers. Many fashion designers who start as assistant designers become head designers. Experienced designers in large firms may advance to chief designer, design department head, or other supervisory positions. Designers in these positions oversee less experienced designers.

Fashion designers who want to advance should stay prepared. They should keep updated portfolios to show employers, clients, and other

Designers have a variety of advancement opportunities.

contacts. Fashion designers also should be aware of jobs at other firms. Some fashion designers advance to better jobs at other design firms.

Experienced designers can advance in a variety of ways. Some become partners in the design firm or apparel company at which they work. Others may open their own design firm, retail shop, or freelance business. Designers with these types of jobs are self-employed.

Experienced fashion designers may start their own design companies.

A few experienced designers may create their own line or label. Some designers may start their own design companies. Other designers may develop their own label for a large company.

Related Careers

Many job opportunities are available for people interested in design or fashion. They may become fashion consultants or product buyers. Clients pay fashion consultants to help them select clothes to wear. Product buyers select clothes or accessories for stores to sell.

People who are interested in art and design have a variety of job opportunities. Some become interior decorators, graphic designers, or floral designers. Clients hire interior decorators to help them decorate their homes or businesses. Graphic designers create graphic items for advertisements, product packages, and cards. Floral designers create floral arrangements. Other people interested in design and art may become architects or photographers. Architects design buildings and other structures.

Each design area involves specialized training. People trained to be floral designers may not be good interior decorators.

The fashion industry changes as people's ideas about fashion change. People will want new clothes and accessories as their fashion tastes change. Fashion designers will be needed to create new and interesting styles and designs to meet these needs.

Words to Know

collection (kuh-LEK-shuhn)—a group of designs created by a fashion designer

croquis (kro-KE)—a small rough sketch used by designers during the design process

garment (GAR-muhnt)—a piece of clothing

gouache (GWASH)—a type of paint used to color sketches

merchandising (MUR-chuhn-dize-ing)—the process of selling items such as clothing or accessories

portfolio (port-FOH-lee-oh)—a set of pictures or designs either bound in book form or loose in a folder; fashion designers collect samples of their work in their portfolios.

sketch (SKECH)—a quick, rough drawing of a garment or accessory design

textile (TEK-stile)—a fabric or cloth that is woven or knitted

trend (TREND)—the latest fashion

To Learn More

Cosgrove, Holli, ed. *Career Discovery Encyclopedia.* Vol. 3. 4th ed. Chicago: Ferguson Publishing, 2000.

Dolber, Roslyn. *Opportunities in Fashion Careers.* VGM Opportunities. Lincolnwood, Ill.: VGM Career Horizons, 1993.

Gardner, Elizabeth B. *Opportunities in Arts and Crafts Careers.* VGM Opportunities. Lincolnwood, Ill.: VGM Career Horizons, 1999.

Mauro, Lucia. *Careers for Fashion Plates and Other Trendsetters.* VGM Careers For You. Lincolnwood, Ill.: VGM Career Horizons, 1996.

Tain, Linda. *Portfolio Presentation for Fashion Designers.* New York: Fairchild, 1997.

Useful Addresses

Council of Fashion Designers of America
1412 Broadway
Suite 2006
New York, NY 10018

The Fashion Group International
597 Fifth Avenue
Eighth Floor
New York, NY 10017

International Apparel Federation
5 Portland Place
London W1N 3AA
England

**National Association of Schools of Art and
Design**
11250 Roger Bacon Drive
Suite 21
Reston, VA 20190

Internet Sites

The Fashion Group International
http://www.fgi.org

Fashion Institute of Design and Merchandising
http://www.fidm.com

The Fashion Institute of Technology
http://www.fitnyc.suny.edu

The Internet Centre for Canadian Fashion and Design
http://www.ntgi.net/ICCF%26D/index2.htm

Job Futures—Creative Designers and Craftspersons
http://www.hrdc-drhc.gc.ca/corp/stratpol/arb/
    jobs/english/volume1/524/524.htm

Occupational Outlook Handbook—Designers
http://stats.bls.gov/oco/ocos090.htm

Index